MAR 0 2 2006

Childhoods
of the
Presidents

Bill Clinton

Childhoods
of the
Presidents

John Adams

George W. Bush

Bill Clinton

Ulysses S. Grant

Andrew Jackson

Thomas Jefferson

John F. Kennedy

Abraham Lincoln

James Madison

James Monroe

Ronald Reagan

Franklin D. Roosevelt

Theodore Roosevelt

Harry S. Truman

George Washington

Woodrow Wilson

Bill Clinton

Hal Marcovitz

Mason Crest Publishers
Philadelphia

Produced by OTTN Publishing, Stockton, New Jersey

Mason Crest Publishers
370 Reed Road
Broomall, PA 19008
www.masoncrest.com

3 5 7 9 8 6 4 2

Library of Congress Cataloging-in-Publication Data

Marcovitz, Hal.
    Bill Clinton / Hal Marcovitz.
        p.   cm.   (Childhood of the presidents)
    Summary: A biography of the forty-second president of the
    United States, focusing on his childhood and young adulthood.
    Includes bibliographical references and index.
        ISBN 1-59084-273-1
    1. Clinton, Bill, 1946-   —Childhood and youth—Juvenile litera-
    ture. 2. Clinton, Bill, 1946-   —Juvenile literature. 3. Presidents—
    United States—Biography—Juvenile literature. [1. Clinton, Bill,
    1946-   —Childhood and youth. 2. Presidents.] I. Title.
    II. Series.
    E886.2.M364 2003
    973.929'092—dc21
    [B]   2002069236

Publisher's note: All quotations in this book come from
original sources, and contain the spelling and grammatical
inconsistencies of the original text.

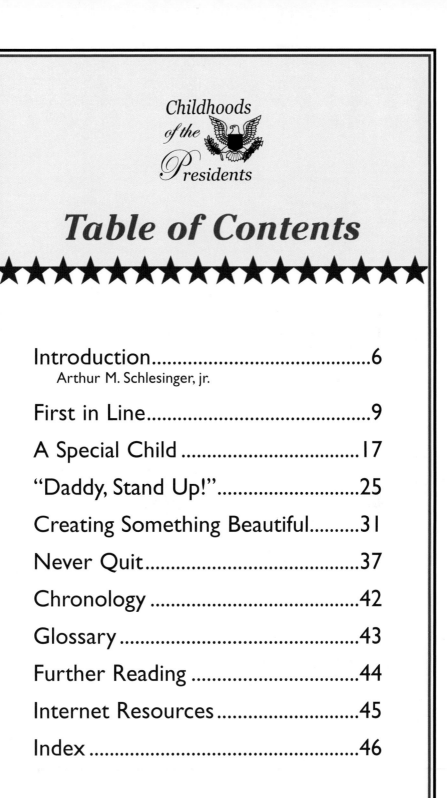

Childhoods
of the
Presidents

Table of Contents

★★★★★★★★★★★★★★★★

★ *Introduction* ★

Alexis de Tocqueville began his great work *Democracy in America* with a discourse on childhood. If we are to understand the prejudices, the habits and the passions that will rule a man's life, Tocqueville said, we must watch the baby in his mother's arms; we must see the first images that the world casts upon the mirror of his mind; we must hear the first words that awaken his sleeping powers of thought. "The entire man," he wrote, "is, so to speak, to be seen in the cradle of the child."

That is why these books on the childhoods of the American presidents are so much to the point. And, as our history shows, a great variety of childhoods can lead to the White House. The record confirms the ancient adage that every American boy, no matter how unpromising his beginnings, can aspire to the presidency. Soon, one hopes, the adage will be extended to include every American girl.

All our presidents thus far have been white males who, within the limits of their gender, reflect the diversity of American life. They were born in nineteen of our states; eight of the last thirteen presidents were born west of the Mississippi. Of all our presidents, Abraham Lincoln had the least promising childhood, yet he became our greatest president. Oddly enough, presidents who are children of privilege sometimes feel an obligation to reform society in order to give children of poverty a better break. And, with Lincoln the great exception, presidents who are children of poverty sometimes feel that there is no need to reform a society that has enabled them to rise from privation to the summit.

Does schooling make a difference? Harry S. Truman, the only twentieth-century president never to attend college, is generally accounted a near-great president. Actually nine— more than one fifth—of our presidents never went to college at all, including such luminaries as George Washington, Andrew Jackson and Grover Cleveland. But, Truman aside, all the non-college men held the highest office before the twentieth century, and, given the increasing complexity of life, a college education will unquestionably be a necessity in the twenty-first century.

Every reader of this book, girls included, has a right to aspire to the presidency. As you survey the childhoods of those who made it, try to figure out the qualities that brought them to the White House. I would suggest that among those qualities are ambition, determination, discipline, education— and luck.

—ARTHUR M. SCHLESINGER, JR.

President John F. Kennedy shakes hands with a 16-year-old from Arkansas, 1963. Thirty years later, that young man, Bill Clinton, would himself occupy the White House—and his intelligence, charisma, and vigor would remind many people of Kennedy.

First in Line

When African-American soldiers from Arkansas returned home in 1945 after fighting in World War II, they found the same racism that had been a part of life in the South before the war. Blacks were not permitted to eat in the same restaurants as whites. They could not use the same public bathroom facilities or drink from the same water fountains. They were expected to give up their bus seats to white riders, and their children were not permitted to attend the same schools as white students.

Even after the United States Supreme Court made a number of rulings establishing civil rights for African Americans, equality was slow to come to the state of Arkansas. In 1957, the school board in the Arkansas capital of Little Rock opened the doors of Little Rock High School to nine black students. But Governor Orval Faubus swore that black students would never enter the school, and he dispatched the Arkansas National Guard to keep them out. Only after President Dwight D. Eisenhower stepped in and ordered the National Guard to leave Little Rock were the black students permitted to enter.

Growing up amid this racial tension in Arkansas was Bill Clinton. Born just after World War II, he was raised first in Hope, a tiny town not far from the Texas border, and then in Hot Springs, a much larger community about 80 miles north of Hope. But wherever he went, Bill Clinton couldn't help but notice that blacks and whites were not treated equally. The boy soon concluded that treatment of blacks in Arkansas and elsewhere in the South was unfair.

"He was seeing black people mistreated in school," said his mother, Virginia Clinton Kelley, "and he felt then it was just because of their color; and he just could hardly stand it."

Although the Clintons were certainly not racial reformers, the family was far more tolerant of blacks than were their neighbors. Bill's grandmother, Edith Cassidy, worked as a nurse in Hope, and she would often drive into the black section of town to see patients who had no money for medical care. Her husband Eldridge, who owned a grocery store on the edge of the white section of Hope, was always willing to accept blacks as customers.

When Bill Clinton was 16 years old, he was picked by the American Legion post in Hot Springs to attend the Arkansas convention for Boys Nation. The American Legion is an organization of *veterans*, and it sponsors many activities designed to help students learn about the government of America. Boys Nation was one such activity. Two "senators" from each state would be selected at their conventions to attend a national convention in Washington. There they would spend a week learning about the federal government, visiting the historic landmarks in the nation's capital, and actually passing *resolu-*

The Arkansas of Bill Clinton's childhood was a racially troubled place. In 1957, when Bill was 11, black students were first admitted to Little Rock High School—but only after President Eisenhower had dispatched federal troops. In 1997 President Clinton attended a 40th anniversary celebration of the school's integration.

tions that would take positions on the important issues of the day. The resolutions would be adopted through votes by the senators, and the sponsors of Boys Nation hoped that the students would engage in vigorous debates on the resolutions so they could experience the true nature of *lawmaking*.

But to take part in Boys Nation, Bill Clinton would have to win the job of senator at the Arkansas convention. In late June, Bill attended the state convention at a summer camp near Little Rock. He spent the week campaigning hard for the job, going from cabin to cabin each night so he could introduce himself to the hundreds of other boys in attendance. In the morning, he rose early so he could station himself at the

The 1963 Boys Nation senators were deeply divided over the issue of civil rights for African Americans. Bill Clinton (first row, third from right) staunchly supported a resolution calling for racial equality—and he stood up to other senators from the South to see that it passed.

entrance of the cafeteria and shake hands with the boys as they arrived for breakfast. He recruited many friends at the camp, and they fanned out and urged their friends to vote for Bill Clinton for Boys Nation senator.

By the end of the week every boy at the state convention had met Bill. Most liked the eager young man, who impressed them with his intelligence, drive, and ability to make friends. He won the election in a *landslide*.

"It's the biggest thrill and honor of my life," he said after winning the election. "I hope I can do the tremendous job required of me as a representative of the state. I hope I can live up to the task."

Bill Clinton and the other Arkansas senator, Larry Taunton, left for Boys Nation on July 19, 1963. It would be one of the hottest weeks of the year in the nation's capital. The 100 boys attending Boys Nation stayed that week in dormitories at the University of Maryland. Their days were filled with trips to *cabinet* departments, lunches with members of *Congress*, and sessions to draft resolutions that would be placed before all 100 Boys Nation senators for a vote.

By the summer of 1963, the issue of civil rights for African Americans was still very much in dispute. In 1962, President John F. Kennedy had been forced to send U.S. marshals to Mississippi so that a black student, James Meredith, could be admitted to the all-white University of Mississippi. Eight months later, Kennedy had sent U.S. marshals as well as federal troops to the University of Alabama to ensure that two black students would be permitted to enroll there.

At Boys Nation, the senators drafted a resolution supporting civil rights for African Americans. As a senator from a southern state, Bill Clinton was expected to vote against the resolution—just as the majority of adult politicians from the South were trying to block racial equality. But Bill had no intentions of opposing the resolution. In fact, he was one of the major voices for civil rights at the convention. He worked hard on the convention floor rounding up votes for the civil rights resolution, using the same political skills that had won him votes just a few weeks before at the state convention in Little Rock.

He found strong opposition on the convention floor. Two of the southern senators—Pete Johnson of Alabama and

Tommy Lawhorne of Georgia—were committed to defeating the civil rights resolution. One morning, they confronted Bill in the University of Maryland cafeteria. They told him that all the southern senators had to stick together at the convention to defeat the civil rights resolution. Soon, Bill Clinton and the other two boys were shouting at one another. Bill refused to budge, though, and Johnson and Lawhorne had to back off.

The civil rights resolution passed by a small margin. The resolution written by Bill Clinton and the other senators favoring civil rights read: "Racial discrimination is a cancerous disease and must be eliminated. Legislation alone can't change the hearts and minds of men. Education is the primary tool which we must employ. It must begin in the home, in the church and in the schools."

The next morning, Bill Clinton and the other Boys Nation senators were to board buses on the University of Maryland campus for what was to be the final activity of their week in Washington: a tour of the White House and a meeting on the White House lawn with President Kennedy.

When the other boys showed up to board the buses, they found Bill already standing in line. He arrived first because he intended to sit in the front seat of the first bus, so that he could be first off the bus. That way, Bill hoped, he could be first to meet the president.

In Hot Springs, Bill Clinton's next-door neighbor and friend Carolyn Yelldell went to Girls Nation the same year Bill went to Boys Nation. She met President John F. Kennedy at the conclusion of her convention, too.

When the buses arrived at the White House, Bill leaped out of his seat and hurried to the front of the line. He found a place just to the right of where President Kennedy was expected to stand to greet the boys.

> **Bill Clinton won his first election when he was 15 years old. He was voted president of the sophomore class at Hot Springs High School.**

Just before 10 o'clock in the morning, Kennedy stepped out of the White House to address the 100 Boys Nation senators. He told them that he had read a newspaper story that morning about their convention, and he was particularly impressed with their resolution calling for civil rights.

Kennedy then talked about the White House, explaining that it had opened during the presidency of John Adams. Although it had changed over the years, the president said, the White House had always remained a symbol of America. He said, "So all around you is the story of the United States and I think all of us have a pride in our country."

When he concluded his speech, the president stepped forward and extended his hand to greet the Boys Nation senators. The first hand he shook was Bill Clinton's. The 16-year-old from Arkansas had planned to say a few words to the president, but on this morning in Washington he was completely speechless.

Nearly 30 years later, Bill Clinton would be elected president of the United States. And he would never again find himself at a loss for words.

William Jefferson Blythe III (seen here at about 18 months) was a precocious child who learned to read before turning three. Bill, whose father died before his birth, would later take the last name of his stepfather, Roger Clinton.

A Special Child

ugust 18 was recorded as the hottest day of 1946 in the tiny southwestern Arkansas town of Hope. That day, the temperature hit 101 degrees. Arkansans are used to their hot and steamy summers, but few of them could remember when a day in Hope had been so uncomfortable.

The heat spell was broken when a violent thunderstorm blew through town that night. Explosive cracks of lightning and window-rattling booms of thunder kept people awake.

It is unlikely that Virginia Blythe would have gotten much sleep, anyway. On that night, Virginia was in *labor* in her parents' home on Hervey Street in Hope.

"I lay awake in my bed and listened for the crash of thunder and counted the seconds until the lightning slashed through the sky; usually, I didn't have to count long," Virginia said. "Dear lord, please don't let it hit this house."

Soon, the storm passed. Monday, August 19, 1946, turned out to be a beautiful, sun-kissed day in Hope. At dawn Virginia's father, Eldridge Cassidy, drove his daughter to Julia Chester Hospital in Hope. Virginia's son, William Jefferson Blythe III, was born at 8:51 that morning.

Bill Clinton's boyhood home in Hope, a small town in southwestern Arkansas.

His father, Bill Blythe, had died three months before in a car accident. Virginia met and married Blythe during World War II while she was training as a nurse in Louisiana and he was preparing to enlist in the army. When Blythe arrived home from the war in late 1945, he found a job as a salesman in Chicago, Illinois. The Blythes briefly lived in an apartment in Chicago, but when Virginia became pregnant she decided to move back with her parents in Arkansas while Bill searched for a house in Chicago. On one of his trips home to see Virginia a tire on his car blew out, causing the vehicle to roll over. He was found dead in a ditch near the wreck of his car.

Bill Blythe III may have been born into a home without a father, but he never wanted for love. Virginia's mother, Edith Cassidy, was especially fond of the boy, taking delight in feeding him, picking out his clothes, and overseeing his playtime. It was Edith Cassidy who first recognized his intelligence. Under her guidance, Bill learned to read before he was three years old. Usually, children start reading at five or six.

"From the beginning, Bill was a special child—smart, sensitive, mature beyond his years," recalled Virginia. "He remembers my sitting him down in that house and telling him about his real father. He must have been 4 or 5 at the time, but talking with him at that age was like talking with a grown friend."

Meanwhile, Virginia met Roger Clinton, the owner of a car dealership in Hope. Roger loved to drink liquor, gamble, and spend his nights roaming the bars of Hope in search of fun. But Virginia thought she could tame his wild spirit. They were married on June 19, 1950. Roger and Virginia Clinton and Virginia's son, Bill, moved into a small house on Thirteenth Street in Hope.

Virginia found that she was unable to keep her new husband home. He still liked to drink, gamble, and enjoy the nightlife. Virginia was determined to provide for her family, though. She had trained as a nurse during the war and found work with some doctors in Hope.

Hope, Arkansas, is named for Hope Loughborough, the daughter of a railroad company executive who drew up the original plans for the city.

Virginia enrolled her boy in school under the name of Bill Clinton. From early on, he impressed his teachers with his intelligence and zeal to learn. Some of his teachers weren't quite sure what to make of the little boy who always knew the answers in class. In the second grade, he raised his hand so much that his teacher regarded him as a pest and gave him a D in behavior.

That was Bill's last poor grade. For the rest of his school years he was an A student who always seemed to be far ahead of his classmates.

Roger Clinton was originally from Hot Springs, and that's where the couple moved in 1952. Bill's stepfather lost money in the car business in Hope and finally decided to give it up and try farming. The family found a farm on the edge of town, but it soon became clear that Roger Clinton was not the type of man who could drag himself out of bed before dawn to milk the cows and feed the hens. Roger enjoyed the nightlife too much to keep farmers' hours. Virginia had no intentions of becoming a farm wife, either. By now she had become an *anesthetist*, and she found her skills very much in demand by Hot Springs surgeons. She was one of only three anesthetists in town.

A replica of Bill Clinton's first home on Hervey Street in Hope, Arkansas, has been erected on the Japanese island of Okinawa. The replica was built to welcome the president during a visit to the island in July 2000.

Bill hated the farm. Virginia recalled the time he was attacked by a ram during a family picnic.

"Suddenly, I heard the children screaming, and I ran outside, Roger and the others

Christmas morning at the Clinton house. Young Bill seems delighted with his presents.

right behind me," she said. "When I saw what was happening, I almost died of fright. A big ram had Bill down, and every time he would try to get up the ram would butt him again. The ram had the most gigantic head I had ever seen. Bill was screaming for help, but we all just stood there with our mouths open; it was as though we were paralyzed and couldn't make our bodies do what needed to be done."

Bill was saved when his grandfather Al Clinton killed the animal by smashing it in the head with a rock.

After just a few months on the farm the Clintons moved to a home on Park Avenue in Hot Springs. Roger Clinton found a job as a salesman.

Bill continued to thrive in school. One of his favorite classes at Ramble Elementary School in Hot Springs was music. Bill enjoyed singing the folk songs the young music teacher taught in class, and he particularly enjoyed the song "Froggie Went A-Courtin' " because the teacher would sing a duet with the student she picked to perform in front of the class.

"Miss Mousie, will you marry me?" Bill would sing to his teacher.

"Without my Uncle Rat's consent I would not marry the pres-i-dent," the teacher would sing back.

Back home, Virginia and Roger were growing apart. Virginia did her best to raise Bill in a normal and happy home, but Roger would come home drunk and get into terrible fights

Bill Clinton's mother, Virginia, holds a photo of her two sons. A desire to be closer to his half-brother, Roger, motivated the 15-year-old Bill to legally change his last name.

with his wife. Bill's mother often seemed ready to end her marriage to Roger, but deep down she always found a way to continue loving him. In 1956, she gave birth to a baby boy. For the time being, at least, it seemed as though there was a reason for Virginia and Roger to stay married.

Roger Cassidy Clinton was the boy's name. He was 10 years younger than his half-brother, Bill. Even with the age difference, Bill found a true friend in his little brother and formed a bond with Roger that would last into their adult years.

When Bill was 15 years old, his mother received a phone call from a judge in the courthouse in Hot Springs. "Virginia," the judge said, "Bill's in my office."

At first, Virginia thought the judge was calling because her eldest son had gotten into some trouble. But that wasn't the reason. For almost his entire life, the boy had gone under the name of Bill Clinton even though his stepfather, Roger Clinton, had never adopted him. Now, the judge explained, Bill wanted to change his last name legally from Blythe to Clinton.

Virginia told the judge that if that's what Bill wanted to do, he had her approval to change his name.

When he returned home from the courthouse, Virginia asked Bill why he wanted to change his name. Bill explained to her that he wished to form a closer bond with his half-brother, and that true brothers share a last name.

He said: "A man's name doesn't make any difference in the world, Mother. It's the man."

ambers, Ernest   Chambers, Kathy   Chambers,

mons, Loyd   Clinton, Billy   Coburn, Fay

By the time this high school yearbook photo was taken, Bill Clinton had confronted his abusive stepfather—a turning point in Bill's early life.

"Daddy, Stand Up!"

*T*he town of Hot Springs owes its name to the heated waters that rise to the top of nearby Hot Springs Mountain. Forty-seven springs make their way down the mountain to the town below. The water in the springs is naturally heated to a temperature of 147 degrees.

The water in the springs is believed to be more than 4,000 years old. Many centuries ago, heavy rain in the Arkansas forests seeped down miles below the surface. Heat from the earth's core makes the water rise again to the top, where it emerges on Hot Springs Mountain. More than a million gallons of hot water a day flow down the mountain.

Many people with *arthritis* and similar physical ailments believe the springs have healing powers. Since the 1800s, visitors have flocked to Hot Springs to bathe in the waters, making the town a popular resort. In the early days, the government of the town fell under the control of powerful criminals who aimed to make money from the springs. The crime leaders built bathhouses for people to enjoy the heated waters. Along with the bathhouses came hotels, nightclubs, and *casinos*. During the *Prohibition* years in the 1920s and early 1930s, the sale of alcohol was illegal in the United States—but in Hot Springs police were paid not to enforce the drinking laws. For years, casino gambling was illegal in most places in America, including Hot Springs. But again, local police turned a blind eye to it all.

By the time Roger and Virginia Clinton moved to Hot Springs, the crime leaders had been kicked out by reform-minded citizens. Still, efforts to tone down the nightlife in town had not yet been successful.

For Roger Clinton, the temptation of the wild nightlife in Hot Springs was too much to resist. When he was sober, Virginia and Bill found him to be a charming man dedicated to the welfare of his family. But when he drank, which was almost every day, Roger Clinton became an angry and jealous husband who often flew into rages at his wife, accusing her of seeing other men.

"At around suppertime I would always be in the kitchen with Bill, and we would hear Roger's car drive up," Virginia said. "As soon as those sound waves reached my ears, I would begin to tense up and I could tell Bill would, too. The car door would slam, and we would hear footsteps crunching across the gravel. As Roger got almost to the door, we could hear him cursing to himself. At times like that, I knew we were in for a night of it."

Years later, Virginia and Bill would often tell people about the good qualities of Roger Clinton, the qualities that shone through when he wasn't drinking. Even though Bill was not his natural child, Roger showed a love for the boy, and Bill responded. When Bill was very young Roger bought him a

Hot Springs (pictured here: Central Avenue opposite the historic Bathhouse Row) provided an irresistible temptation for Roger Clinton, who went on frequent drinking binges in the city's bars and nightclubs. Afterward, he often became abusive toward his wife— once even firing a pistol at her.

Lionel train set. Roger and his stepson would lock themselves in the playroom for hours, playing with the electric trains. Bill had no second thoughts about calling Roger "Daddy."

Sadly, those wonderful experiences were few and far between. Roger's *alcoholism* brought out the worst in his character. Once, when Bill was five years old, Virginia was preparing to visit her grandmother in the hospital. As she was leaving, a drunken Roger confronted her, demanding to know why she was going out. When she told him, he didn't believe her and the two started arguing. Suddenly, Roger reached for a gun and fired it at his wife.

The bullet missed, striking a bedroom wall.

"I grabbed Bill by the hand and we got out of there," Virginia said. "We went across the street to the neighbors' house and they called the police. In a few minutes a squad car

Bill Clinton's life journey would take him from Hope to Hot Springs to the Arkansas governor's mansion in Little Rock before his emergence as a national political figure.

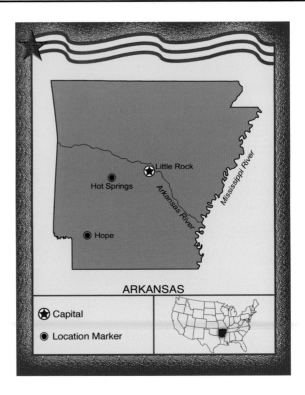

ARKANSAS

★ Capital

◉ Location Marker

pulled up in front of my house and two policemen knocked on the door and arrested Roger."

Roger spent the night in jail. Virginia said she would take him back only if he stopped drinking. Roger agreed, but soon he broke his promise.

Drawn back to the Hot Springs nightlife, Roger would return home after long bouts of drinking to abuse his family. Although he never again picked up a gun, he began striking Virginia. For years, Virginia and her two sons lived under the constant terror of Roger's drunken rages. Finally, when Bill was 14 years old, he aimed to stop it. By now, he was taller than his stepfather and weighed more than 200 pounds.

For hours, Roger and Virginia had been shouting at each other. Bill was in his bedroom, but he could not ignore the argument. He found them in the kitchen. Roger was slumped in a chair, worn out from the hours of bickering.

"Daddy, stand up!" Bill demanded.

Roger didn't have the strength to stand up. He drunkenly mumbled a few words.

"You must stand up to hear what I have to say to you," Bill demanded. "Daddy, I want you on your feet."

Roger stared blankly at his stepson.

"If you can't stand up, I'll help you," Bill said.

Bill lifted Roger from his seat and held him as the older man stood on wobbly legs. "Hear me," he said to Roger. "Never, ever, touch my mother again."

Roger Clinton died of cancer in 1967. By then, Bill had left for college at Georgetown University in Washington, D.C. During the final few weeks of his stepfather's life, Bill Clinton found the strength in his heart to forgive him. Roger Clinton was hospitalized at Duke University in North Carolina. Bill made several trips down from Washington to stay with him.

Just days before Roger Clinton died, Bill obtained permission from the doctors to take his stepfather for a drive around the city of Chapel Hill. "We saw all the dogwoods," Bill said. "It was stunningly beautiful. It was one of the most beautiful days I can ever remember in my entire life. And it was a wonderful experience we had, just the two of us."

In 1968, while attending Georgetown University in Washington, D.C., Bill Clinton painted a red cross on his car and brought food to neighborhoods where race rioting had driven off grocery delivery trucks.

4

Bill Clinton mugs it up for a high school graduation day photo. During his time at Hot Springs High, he had excelled both academically and as a musician.

Creating Something Beautiful

On August 16, 1977, Virginia Clinton received a call from her son Bill. Virginia was at a hospital in Hot Springs, preparing a patient for surgery.

"My children never, ever called me in the operating room," said Virginia. "They were just cautioned it was not the place to call me ever, unless it was an emergency. And so Bill called and he said, 'Please take the phone to Mother. I have something to say to her that I don't want anybody else to tell her.' And he told me Elvis was dead. Oh, what a shock, what a shock."

A lot of people in America were shocked that day to hear of the death of Elvis Presley, perhaps the most famous rock 'n' roll singer who ever lived. Bill and Roger Cassidy Clinton had grown up listening to the songs of Presley, who was especially dear to his fans in the South because he had been born and raised in Tupelo, Mississippi. In the Clinton home, a bust of Elvis Presley sat on a living room table for years.

The Clintons loved music, and both Bill and his brother, Roger, were accomplished musicians. Roger formed his own rock 'n' roll band and became a professional singer. Bill learned to play the saxophone and was considered by his teachers to be good enough to turn professional himself.

Bill took up the saxophone while his mother was still married to Roger Clinton. Playing the instrument was a way to fill his time when he locked himself in his room to get away from his mother and stepfather's constant bickering. While Roger and Virginia argued in the kitchen below, Bill would fill his room with the tones and rhythms he produced from the instrument. The saxophone, he said, gave him "the opportunity to create something that was beautiful, something that I could channel my sensitivity, my feelings into."

As he grew older Bill learned to sight-read music, meaning he could take a piece of music he'd never seen before and play the notes perfectly the first time. What's more, he was a good improviser—he could take what the composer had written and add his own touches to the music while playing.

When Bill arrived at Hot Springs High School, the music teacher and band director, Virgil Spurlin, quickly recognized his talent. Spurlin appointed Bill the band major—a job that went to the band's most accomplished musician. But Spurlin had an interest in the young saxophone player for another reason: he noticed Bill's intelligence, popularity, and organizing skills. These qualities would be a great help to Spurlin in organizing the annual Arkansas statewide band competition, which Hot Springs High School hosted.

It was an incredibly difficult and tedious job. The festival featured performances by 140 high school bands from throughout Arkansas. As head of the festival, Spurlin had to take care of hundreds of details: hiring dozens of judges and

As a teenager, Bill Clinton enjoyed eating at hamburger stands like the Polar Bear and Bailey's in Hot Springs. His favorite meal was a chili cheeseburger, french fries, and grape soda.

finding rooms for them in Hot Springs hotels, leasing 40 pianos for the visiting bands, and scheduling hundreds of performances, not only at the high school but in hotel ballrooms and music schools throughout Hot Springs.

Spurlin and Bill Clinton would cover a wall in the high school with poster boards, then start writing in the names of bands, the places they were scheduled to play, and the judges who would be assigned to hear them. Not only did all 140 bands play in the competition, but each band also featured solo and ensemble performers as well. Each soloist and ensemble would be assigned a place on the wall.

During the three days of the festival each spring, music fans in Hot Springs as well as the thousands of parents who attended the festival had their choice of some 10 performances each hour.

Bill worked hard to help Spurlin coordinate the festival while still finding time to practice and compete with the Hot Springs High School band himself. He also joined the Stardusters, the Hot Springs dance band. And Bill and two of his friends formed a jazz combo that played in the high school cafeteria during lunch hour. They wore dark sunglasses, which prompted their classmates to call the group the Three Blind Mice. At home, the wall of Bill's bedroom displayed the numerous medals and awards he received for winning saxophone competitions. By the time he entered his senior year in high school, he was being urged by teachers to major in music at college.

As a presidential candidate, Bill Clinton entertained potential voters with his saxophone playing. Years before, while in high school, the talented musician had won statewide competitions and had even toyed with the idea of pursuing a career in music.

Spurlin recalled, "One time down in Camden, Arkansas, I believe he was in a stage band, and he was a soloist, and he received the outstanding soloist for the state in this particular case. And it wasn't just the fact that he was an accomplished musician, but he had to read music of all kinds of moods and different kinds of music, from jazz to classical to everything in the book, and he just did a phenomenal job in that. He's the only one in my band who ever received such distinction."

For the teenaged Bill Clinton, the idea of a career in music held great appeal. In 1956, Elvis Presley had become an international star when he appeared on *The Ed Sullivan Show*. At home, Bill and his brother would hurry home from school so they could turn on the TV and watch the popular music show *American Bandstand*. In England, a rock 'n' roll band named the Beatles was starting to make headlines.

Nevertheless, after Bill Clinton was picked to attend Boys Nation in the summer of 1963, and after he met President Kennedy, his mind was made up: he would pursue a career in politics and government, not music. But he never gave up his love for the saxophone.

In 1992, when he first ran for president, Bill Clinton appeared on *The Arsenio Hall Show*, a music and comedy program. He shocked the nation—and, perhaps, won some votes—when he put on dark sunglasses, picked up his saxophone, and belted out a melody. The song he selected was "Heartbreak Hotel." It had been one of Elvis Presley's greatest hits.

> As president, Clinton would occasionally amuse the White House press corps with his dead-on Elvis impersonation.

Never Quit

Whe hen Bill Clinton returned home after completing his education in 1974, he wasted little time getting started on a career in politics and government. In 1976, he won election as attorney general in Arkansas. As attorney general, he was responsible for enforcing all laws in the state. Two years later, the voters elected him governor of Arkansas. At 32 years old, he was the youngest governor in the nation.

It had been a swift climb for the young man from Hope and Hot Springs. Following high school, Bill Clinton enrolled at Georgetown University in Washington, D.C. He picked the college because of its location in the nation's capital—he figured it would be best to study government in the seat of the federal government. After Georgetown, he won a *scholarship* to study in England, then enrolled at Yale Law School in Connecticut in 1971. At Yale, he met a law student from Chicago named Hillary Rodham.

The 42nd president and First Lady Hillary Rodham Clinton at a White House ceremony, May 2000. A close adviser of her husband throughout his political career, Mrs. Clinton herself entered politics by running for, and winning, a seat in the U.S. Senate in 2000.

Hillary recalled first seeing Bill in the Yale library. Each day, she said, they would sit on different sides of the room and steal glances at each other.

"I decided this was ridiculous," Hillary said, "so I got up and walked up to him and I said, 'You know, if you're going to keep looking at me and I'm going to keep looking back, we at least ought to know each other."

They married in 1975. After law school, they both worked for a brief time in Washington. Then they moved to Arkansas, where Bill found a job teaching at the University of Arkansas while he planned his first political campaign. He failed in that campaign—a race for Congress—but in 1976 won the position of state attorney general. His career was on its way.

There were setbacks, though. In 1980, after serving his first term as governor, Clinton lost his bid for reelection. Voters were angry because he raised the fees people paid to obtain their automobile licenses, using the extra money to fund improvements in Arkansas schools. After the campaign,

In 1978, at the age of 32, Bill Clinton became the youngest governor in the United States.

Clinton admitted that he had rushed the plan through. Although the Arkansas schools were desperately in need of money, he knew that he should have been more patient when making changes.

In 1982 he promised the voters he would take things slower. They responded by making him governor again.

"What I have seen happen to Bill is he has learned the fine art of compromise," said Bev Lindsey, a longtime friend. "And not compromise out of a sense of fear, but out of a sense of strength."

During the 1980s, his success in governing Arkansas came to the attention of national political leaders. In 1988, he was asked to make a major speech at the Democratic National Convention. This is a meeting of party leaders held every four years to select the Democratic *nominee* for president. The party's nominee, Massachusetts governor Michael Dukakis, failed to win the election that fall. But the young governor from Arkansas gained notice as a rising star in the Democratic Party.

Four years later, in 1992, Bill Clinton won his party's nomination for president. Then, in the general election, he defeated President George Bush to capture the White House. In 1996, Clinton would be reelected for another term as president.

Bill Clinton's time in the White House was marked by tremendous growth in the American economy. The number of people who were out of work shrank, and after many years of taking in less money than it spent (a situation referred to as a budget *deficit*), the government finally experienced a budget *surplus*.

Meanwhile, Hillary Rodham Clinton became a very active first lady. Not satisfied with simply performing ceremonial jobs, she involved herself in many issues tackled by her husband's administration, particularly the fight to reform America's health care system. (After the Clintons left the White House in 2001, Hillary became a United States senator representing New York State; she was the first former first lady in history to win election herself to a major political office.)

Bill Clinton's administration was also marked by scandal, though. He was only the second president in U.S. history to be impeached. *Impeachment* is the procedure outlined in the U.S. Constitution for removing a president from office if Congress believes he has done something illegal. In President Clinton's case, the issue was whether he had lied when asked questions under oath about his romantic relationship with a young

Bill Clinton worked hard to help resolve the Israeli-Palestinian conflict. Here, as he looks on approvingly, Prime Minister Yitzhak Rabin of Israel and Palestinian leader Yasir Arafat shake hands on the White House lawn, September 13, 1993. Unfortunately, the peace process agreed to then was later derailed.

An extraordinarily gifted politician, President Clinton confounded critics throughout his eight years in the White House. He consistently outmaneuvered congressional Republicans and remained popular with the American people despite a scandal that led to impeachment proceedings against him.

woman who worked in the White House. Clinton had at first denied the relationship but later admitted that it was true.

While a majority of members of the U.S. House of Representatives voted to impeach the president (order him to stand trial in the U.S. Senate), far fewer than the required two-thirds majority of senators voted to convict him and remove him from office. And even while the impeachment proceedings were going on, Clinton remained popular with the American people. He finished his presidency and left office in January 2001.

"If you live long enough, you'll make mistakes," Bill Clinton once said. "But if you learn from them, you'll be a better person. It's how you handle adversity, not how it affects you. The main thing is never quit, never quit, never quit."

CHRONOLOGY

1946 William Jefferson Blythe III is born on August 19; he later changes his last name to Clinton.

1963 Meets President John F. Kennedy while attending Boys Nation in Washington.

1964 Graduates from high school and enrolls at Georgetown University.

1968 Studies on a Rhodes scholarship in London, England.

1971 Enrolls in Yale Law School, meets Hillary Rodham.

1975 Marries Hillary Rodham.

1976 Elected attorney general of Arkansas.

1978 Elected governor of Arkansas; loses reelection in 1980 but wins the position back two years later.

1980 Daughter Chelsea born.

1988 Addresses the Democratic National Convention in Atlanta, Georgia.

1992 Wins election as president; reelected in 1996.

1999 Survives an impeachment battle in Congress.

2000 Hillary Rodham Clinton elected to U.S. Senate representing New York State.

2001 Bill Clinton leaves the White House after two terms, returns to private life.

alcoholism—a disease marked by the need for, and excessive use of, alcoholic drinks.

anesthetist—a person who administers drugs to a patient to dull or eliminate pain during surgery.

arthritis—a disease of the joints that often causes pain during simple activities such as walking or lifting.

cabinet—top advisers to a president; in America, cabinet members head departments such as State, Defense, and Treasury.

casino—a place where money is gambled on games of chance.

Congress—the legislative, or lawmaking, branch of the American government.

deficit—a situation that occurs when a government spends more money than it collects in taxes.

impeachment—the process specified by the U.S. Constitution for the removal from office of presidents or other high elected officials; also, a vote by the House of Representatives to order a president or other official to appear for trial before the U.S. Senate.

labor—a period shortly before childbirth in which many mothers experience pain.

landslide—a one-sided election victory.

lawmaking—the business of creating laws, carried out in the federal government by the U.S. Congress.

nominee—a person selected by a political party to run for president or other high office.

Prohibition—a period in American history, from 1920 to 1933, in which the manufacture or sale of alcoholic beverages was outlawed.

resolution—a formal expression of opinion made by a lawmaking body or similar organization.

scholarship—financial assistance to help an outstanding student attend college or another school.

surplus—an excess of funds that occurs when a government takes in more money from taxes than it spends.

veteran—a person who has returned to civilian life after serving in the armed forces.

FURTHER READING

Allen, Charles F., and Jonathan Portis. *The Comeback Kid: The Life and Career of Bill Clinton.* New York: Birch Lane Press, 1992.

Kelley, Virginia. *Leading with My Heart: My Life.* New York: Simon & Schuster, 1994.

Kelly, Michael. *Bill Clinton.* Philadelphia: Chelsea House Publishers, 1999.

Maraniss, David. *First in His Class: The Biography of Bill Clinton.* New York: Touchstone, 1995.

- http://www.clintonfoundation.org
  The Clinton Foundation

- http://www.whitehouse.gov/history/presidents/bc42.html
  The White House Biography of William Jefferson Clinton

- http://hotsprings.org/
  Historic Hot Springs, Arkansas

- http://www.hotspringsar.com/
  Hot Springs, Arkansas

- http://clinton.senate.gov/
  U.S. Senator Hillary Rodham Clinton

INDEX

INDEX

PICTURE CREDITS

3:	Hulton/Archive/Liaison Images	27:	Dave G. Houser/Houserstock
8:	Hulton/Archive/Liaison Images	28:	© OTTN Publishing
11:	Courtesy of Aristotle Inc.	30:	Hulton/Archive/Liaison Images
12:	Hulton/Archive/Getty Images	33:	Dave G. Houser/Houserstock
16:	Hulton/Archive/Liaison Images	34:	Reuters NewMedia Inc./Corbis
18:	Dave G. Houser/Houserstock	36:	Reuters NewMedia Inc./Corbis
21:	Hulton/Archive/Liaison Images	38:	Hulton/Archive/Liaison Images
22:	Hulton/Archive/Liaison Images	40:	Hulton/Archive/Getty Images
24:	Hulton/Archive/Liaison Images	41:	Hulton/Archive/Liaison Images

Cover photos: all Hulton/Archive/Liaison Images

Contributors

ARTHUR M. SCHLESINGER JR. holds the Albert Schweitzer Chair in the Humanities at the Graduate Center of the City University of New York. He is the author of more than a dozen books, including *The Age of Jackson*; *The Vital Center*; *The Age of Roosevelt* (3 vols.); *A Thousand Days: John F. Kennedy in the White House*; *Robert Kennedy and His Times*; *The Cycles of American History*; and *The Imperial Presidency*. Professor Schlesinger served as Special Assistant to President Kennedy (1961–63). His numerous awards include the Pulitzer Prize for History; the Pulitzer Prize for Biography; two National Book Awards; the Bancroft Prize; and the American Academy of Arts and Letters Gold Medal for History.

HAL MARCOVITZ is a journalist for *The Morning Call*, a newspaper based in Allentown, Pennsylvania. His other books in the CHILDHOODS OF THE PRESIDENTS series include biographies of Theodore Roosevelt, John F. Kennedy, James Monroe, and John Adams. He lives in Chalfont, Pennsylvania, with his wife, Gail, and daughters Ashley and Michelle.